AF620022

Intended Design

A Journey to Self Awareness

A. Todd Jackson

&

Adrianna Gardner

Interior Graphics/Art Credit: La Vita Ru.

ISBN: 978-1-4834-0647-3 (sc)
ISBN: 978-1-4834-0646-6 (e)

Lulu Publishing Services rev. date: 01/16/2014

Contents

“What would you attempt to do if you knew you
could not fail?” Dr. Robert Schuller

“You are today where your thoughts have brought you; you
will be tomorrow where your thoughts take you.”
James Lane Allen

ACKNOWLEDGEMENTS

From Rev. A. Todd Jackson:

I am so thankful for my biggest cheerleaders, my wife, Sonia and children Essence and Joshua that have supported me through this process. I am particularly grateful to Adrianna Gardner for helping me transfer the words from my head to paper. Also, I would like to offer my special thanks to Sangolana Fasemoyin Epega for her wisdom. Last, but not least I thank God for the spirit of my Ancestors.

From Adrianna Gardner:

I would like to thank Reverend A. Todd Jackson for trusting me with responsibility of assisting him on this writing project. I am appreciative of every spiritual teacher I have had who allowed me to live from their wisdom and life experience. I thank God for the support of family and friends and for the ability to use the writing medium as a tool for change.

INTRODUCTION

Imagine that your purpose in life is as unique as a thumbprint. The intricate curvature of its lines and the distinct mark is one of a kind. You are an intelligent blueprint of the Creator: the Master Architect. Birthmarks, snowflakes, and fingerprints are each unique representations of God's design. All are physical manifestations of God's intelligent drawing. Neither of these birthmarks, snowflakes or fingerprints is identical. Each is an expression of the Creator's image.

Similarly, not one person's aim in life is the same. You are one of God's best designs. *Why?* You are a unique design and cannot be replicated. Your life was created with a specific task in mind. The best thing you can do for your life is to know yourself and to know your purpose.

One of the greatest things a person can have is the knowledge of self. The Ancient Egyptians taught in their sacred temples, "Man, Know thyself." This quote has been spoken by many throughout time, but few know its origination or know why it is so significant.

This is similar to Luke 8: 17, "*For there is nothing hidden that will not be disclosed, and nothing concealed that will not be known or brought out into the open.*" The first step to the knowledge of self is simply asking the question.

This Egyptian concept of knowing oneself originated with their ancestors. The Twa people, originating from the region of modern day Rwanda and Burundi of Central Africa, observed nature as detailed in *Signs and Symbols of Primordial Man* by Albert Churchward.

Based upon this observation they knew that there was a power greater than them. The wind blowing on their face originated from a place beyond their control. The red clay dirt that they walked on and that painted the earth had a source.

We see examples of this in the scripture. Adam and Eve in the Garden of Eden under the Tree of Knowledge is a prime example. The Twa knew there was something more powerful than them a power that controlled the setting of the sun and stars.

Isaiah 44:24 ...... I am the Lord, the Maker of all things, who stretches out the heavens, who spreads out the earth by myself...

In every spiritual system there are the first students who are open to seeking knowledge and wisdom.

The Twa asked the questions that have become the foundation for all spiritual systems. Those questions consisted of: *Who am I? Where did I come from? What do I do here? Where do I go when I leave here? What do I do when I get there?* They formulated the age old question from their dialogue within their own mind and spirit –*What is my purpose?*

I am a firm believer that if you ask the question, then God will give you the answer. I write this book with the intention of it being a simple tool to help others find their purpose. Spiritual enlightenment is not an instanteous event, rather an ongoing process. This book serves as a tool on your journey to knowing your true purpose.

In 2004 I began my personal study of comparative religions, which in 2007 led me to travel to Nigeria where I got a close up look at the spiritual systems of the Yoruba people. I spent time in Ijebu, Ondo, Osun, and Oyo states of the southwestern region which was within the Nigerian Rainforest. They have a saying that states: *Ayanmo ni iwa-pele, iwa-pele ni Aynanno.* It means that Destiny is good character. Good Character is destiny. This simply means that when your future is unclear, just do the right thing in the moment and you will be guided toward your fullest potential.

Sister/Brother, life has placed this book in your path because you have a question about how to move your life to the place where God intended it. You may possibly be living your purpose vicariously through what our society says is the life you should have. God has put you on this earth for a reason. We encourage you to use this book to find that reason.

We are certain that God did not put you here for show. I often find that we do ourselves a disservice when we underestimate our personal power and our potential for growth and change. In our careers, lives, and relationships we often sale ourselves short of what is our birthright to attain, experience, and achieve. You have a mission that is unique only to you. The word "intended" in the title of this book signifies *purpose.*

We will take our journey through the Wheel of Life in the pages to follow by asking the question in each quadrant and using the various exercises to reflect and act.

WHEEL OF LIFE

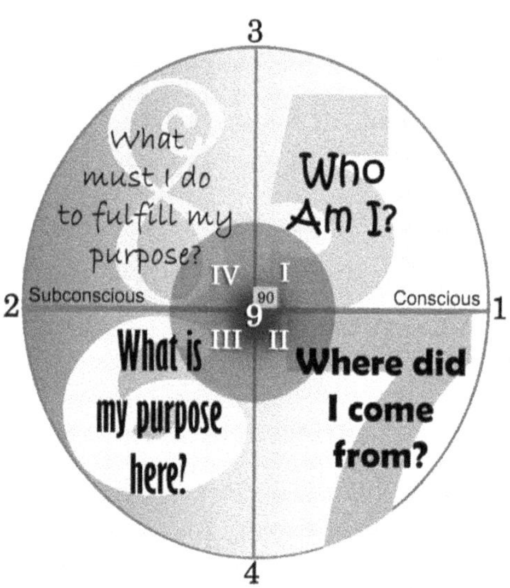

In Quadrant I, we look into the core of your individuality and explore what makes you who you really are. Quadrant II we delve into our past experiences and the influence it has on our present. In Quadrant III, we explore our natural talents and gifts to understand the role they play in pursuing our purpose. Quadrant IV brings all the quadrants together and provides us with a platform to execute our mission on this earth, our purpose.

The journey to introspection and change can be difficult. Be encouraged through quotes placed throughout the book. This is your opportunity to transcend your current situation and transform your life. It is never too late in life to figure out your life's purpose. Fulfilling your purpose is a life-long process. The key to this process is what you do on a daily basis.

Throughout the book, there will be recurring themes between what you work through and what begins to emerge in your life. This is called *synchronicity.*

Keys points to do and to remember when doing any self improvement work:

- Protect your sense of safeness by aligning the exercise within your daily routine. Exclude individuals who are critical or are negative in thought from knowing the details of the journey you are about to embark. Rebuilding yourself takes inner conviction and determination which is undermined by skeptics.
- You are recovering a sense of identity; therefore, be on alert for actions or thoughts that are resistant to change- both internal delays and external roadblocks. These are messages from your subconscious mind—which we will delve into more later in the book.
- Any opportunity to grow comes with mixed emotions. Your personal power is worth regaining. What we do now on a daily basis impacts our long term success.
- Move through this process with integrity by acknowledging some truths about your previous actions. There is a greater possibility of spiritual awakening if you are able take personal responsibility for your present circumstance. There is abundance in love, money, and health to be had once we reclaim our true selves and find our purpose in life.

"There is only one you... Don't you dare change
just because you're outnumbered!"
Charles Swindoll

"We cannot become what we need to be by remaining what we are."
Max De Pree

"It's not what you do once in a while, it's what you do
day in and day out that makes the difference."
Jenny Craig

Let's start our journey with asking the four questions stated above from Quadrant I – IV.

The circle goes clockwise until we have gone 360 degrees. The numbers 1-9 symbolize your personality traits found through nature, those things around you every day that you may pay little or no attention to. We will look closer at them later in the book. We pray that the exercises to follow support, reinforce, and build upon the preceding exercises and techniques that lead to self-mastery.

Exercise:

1. What are your natural gifts and talents? List three things that you would not mind doing for free.

2. Define your Intention Statement.

   For example, *My intention is to use writing as a tool for social change and create a forum for self-awareness. I intend to use my creativity as a medium to encourage self-expression.*

   What do you believe is your life statement?

This will be the foundation for exercises to come and a portion to reflect upon. Return back to this exercise as many times as necessary to determine your Intention Statement.

“The biggest adventure you can ever take is
to live the life of your dreams.”
Oprah Winfrey

“I am not a has-been. I am a will be.”
Lauren Bacall

Quad I

Who am I?

In Quadrant I, we will look into the core of your individuality and explore what makes you who you really are. In life, often time we make the mistake of allowing external things to dictate who we are as individuals. We are more than the car we drive, the house we live in or the people that surround us. Let us take a look at biblical text to give us a picture of what God has to say about how to look within ourselves for answers.

In Exodus 3:1-15, we find the story of Moses—one man that has gone from a man of power and prestige to a man who works a minimum wage job tending his father-in-laws' sheep on top of Mount Horeb. Here we begin our journey in self-awareness. On Mount Horeb God speaks to Moses through the burning bush. He recognizes he is on Holy Ground. Then, he removes his shoes. At the end of the conversation with God, it was instructed for Moses to deliver the message to Pharaoh to let God's people go. Pharaoh was to release Moses' people from slavery. Moses asks God who should he tell them sent him on such a mission. God tells Moses, "I am that I am." These are the most powerful words any person can utter.

This scripture provides us with a framework for how to self reflect. The key points of the story to remember of this parable is that Mount Horeb was a place of solitude – symbolizing meditation or quiet time. Meditation is you closing your eyes and letting go. It is a place that resides within the inner workings of silence. There are many forms of meditation, either sitting or standing. We will not get technical about the type of meditation, but we will stress the need to focus on your breathing. Meditation is stillness and thought suppression. It is a pause in our busy life that allows us to reconnect our physical bodies to the spirit that resides within it.

The burning bush represents the inner consciousness of man, or the Holy Spirit. There is something divine that takes place when we are still, yet aware.

It is likened to sleeping, yet the benefits are far greater because we are at that moment allowing for the Holy Spirit to come in and inspire us and provide tranquility.

The processing of Moses removing his shoes attests to the limitations we as individuals carry with us. It represents that *I can't do this or that because of whatever reason* thought that lingers in our subconscious. In meditation, we allow all the lists of thoughts to pass and cease. The "To Do" list, "Things I Could Be Doing Right Now Instead of Meditating" list, or the "Who I need to Call Back" list are suppressed in order to allow for new thoughts and new inspiration. Holy Ground is whatever space you occupy because whatever space you reserve for spiritual work is sacred and therefore holy.

I am that I am is one of the strongest statements in the human language to utter. It is your declaration to yourself.

Exercise:

1. Begin to incorporate ten to fifteen minutes of some form of meditation into your day. Record your experience.

2. Exercise: *Mirror Work*: Introduce yourself to yourself, using I AM. You are the most fascinating person that you have *never* met. You hear a lot of people tell you who you are but now here is an opportunity to define who you are for yourself.

3. Who are you? Who are you not?

Who are you?	Who are you not?
I Am ____________	I Am not ____________
I Am ____________	I Am not ____________
I Am ____________	I Am not ____________

This next exercise will lead you to your mirror. This may seem awkward in the beginning, but work through it. While looking directly into your eyes, declare positive affirmations of "I Am."

These exercises are essential to reprogramming the subconscious.

There is no shame in going back to fetch it and correct it.
– Akan people of West Africa

Romans 12:2 ...be ye transformed by the renewing of your mind.

QUAD II

WHERE DID I COME FROM?

When we think about where we come from, our first thought is our genealogy, the people who came before us like our parents, our grandparents and our ancestors. While our bloodline is an accurate blueprint of our beginning, let us look at how our mind has shaped us to do things that we don't know why we are doing them. In Quadrant II we delve into our past in order to move forward. We will explore the environmental factors as well as the psychological influences behind our actions.

In Genesis 19 we find the story of Lot and his family fleeing Sodom and Gomorrah and receiving instructions from the angels not to look back. We pick up this anthropomorphic story in verses 24-26.

Genesis 19:24 Then *the Lord rained upon Sodom and upon Gomorrah brimstone and fire from the Lord out of heaven; 25: And he overthrew those cities, and all the plain, and all the inhabitants of the cities, and that which grew upon the ground. 26: But his wife looked back from behind him, and she became a pillar of salt.*

Lot's wife did not follow the directive and when she looked back she turned into a pillar of salt. Salt acts as a preservative which is synonymous to memory. She looked back because of the ties of her emotions and memories to Sodom and Gomorrah. When you decide to make changes in your life, it is the subconscious mind that trips you up.

A flower that is growing in the meadow has a greater chance of flourishing than the one that is growing in the concrete. No matter how great one's potential in life or one's position, environmental factors have the greatest influences in determining our success. The mind is divided into two parts the, conscious and subconscious.

The subconscious mind is where your beliefs and memories are stored. It can not distinguish what is real or what is imaginary. The environment we were raised in has shaped our beliefs of the people that surround us. Bad habits linger in our subconscious and can only be remove by our self-programming.

I know you are asking, *how do I do this?* Mediation is key to reprogramming our subconscious mind and transcending our environmental influences. Remember that you have to suppress old thoughts in order to birth new ones. When a gardener wishes to repot a plant, she uses new soil.

"You have two primary choices in life: to accept conditions as they exist, or accept the responsibility for changing them."

Denis Waitley

"Yesterday is not ours to recover,
but tomorrow is ours to win or to lose."

Lyndon B. Johnson

Exercise

1. Add one affirmation to change your paradigm.

2. The Mirror concept:

   While looking into the mirror, make a list of your bad habits on a sheet of paper.

   On another sheet of paper, make a list of the total opposites of your bad habits.

   Once this is complete, take the paper with the bad habits and burn it while reciting and personalizing Philippians 2:5-6 *the mind that was in Christ Jesus is in me also.*

   The burning of the bad habits is the ritual of letting go to bring in the new habits that will bring you closer to your purpose.

3. Say the positive affirmations to yourself from Quad I, the positive *I am* affirmations.

   Visualize yourself in the positive affirmations. You can do this exercise whenever it is convenient; however, it is most effective to do at night before bed.

4. Identify some of the limiting messages you have received from others and that you have given to yourself.

   ____

   ____

   ____

5. Write a letter in your defense to the person or people who you received those messages from. When you are finished writing it, burn it.

6. Write a letter to a person or people who have encouraged you. Thank them for the upliftment.

Mid-quadrant Assessment:

"Change your thoughts and you change your world."
Norman Vincent Peale

You are the only person on earth who can use your ability.
Zig Ziglar

"What we see depends mainly on what we look for."
Sir John Lubbock

QUAD III

WHAT IS MY PURPOSE HERE?

We have now entered Quadrant III, and by now you have a clear understanding of the importance of meditation and trusting your intuition.

In this section, we will discover how our natural talents are the gateways to determining our purpose. How many times have we told ourselves that if we were not in our present job then we would pursue our true ambitions? Our purpose is in what gives us our pleasure.

Matt 25:14-26
14 "Again, it will be like a man going on a journey, who called
his servants and entrusted his wealth to them. 15 To one he gave
five bags of gold, to another two bags, and to another one bag,
[a] each according to his ability. Then he went on his journey.
16 The man who had received five bags of gold went at once and
put his money to work and gained five bags more. 17 So also, the
one with two bags of gold gained two more. 18 But the man who

had received one bag went off, dug a hole in the ground and hid his master's money.

19 "After a long time the master of those servants returned and settled accounts with them. 20 The man who had received five bags of gold brought the other five. 'Master,' he said, 'you entrusted me with five bags of gold. See, I've gained five more.'
21 "His master replied, 'well done, good and faithful servant! You have been faithful with a few things; I will put you in charge of many things. Come and share your master's happiness!' 22
"The man with two bags of gold also came. 'Master,' he said, 'you entrusted me with two bags of gold; see, I have gained two more.'
23 "His master replied, 'well done, good and faithful servant! You have been faithful with a few things; I will put you in charge of many things. Come and share your master's happiness!' 24
"Then the man who had received one bag of gold came. 'Master,' he said, 'I knew that you are a hard man, harvesting where you have not sown and gathering where you have not scattered seed.

25 So I was afraid and went out and hid your gold in the ground. See, here is what belongs to you.' 26 "His master replied, 'you wicked, lazy servant! So you knew that I harvest where I have not sown and gather where I have not scattered seed?

In Matt 25:14-26, we find the parable of the talents referred to as gold. Everyone is given a talent and/or purpose, but what we do with it is the key. A confident individual understands and uses his or her gifts to enter into greater possibilities. Fear and doubt are our two greatest enemies. They paralyze us.

The servant that had one bag of gold was consumed with fear and doubt, so he did nothing with his lot. The subconscious mind caused his paralysis.

No increase of abundance in any form is possible for a person who buries their talent and does not maximize his or her full potential. Furthermore an individual in such a position never has any clarity to who they really are or what God placed them on this earth to accomplish.

Exercise

I know you may have seen thousands of exercises or read books on how to find your purpose. If you simply meditate on the things you are passionate about, you are closer to finding your purpose than any other tool suggested. In your meditation make a list of ten things from these two questions:

1) What is the thing you love doing without being forced to do it?
2) What do you find the greatest deal of satisfaction in doing?

It comes so easy. You are a quick learner!

1. ______________________________
2. ______________________________
3. ______________________________
4. ______________________________
5. ______________________________
6. ______________________________
7. ______________________________
8. ______________________________
9. ______________________________
10. ______________________________

If possible get someone you trust to tell you ten things that they think you are good at doing. This will help you to do a compare and contrast. Often knowing what we do not like helps us to find those things we love.

List 10 things you don't like.

1. ______________________________
2. ______________________________
3. ______________________________
4. ______________________________
5. ______________________________
6. ______________________________
7. ______________________________
8. ______________________________
9. ______________________________
10. ______________________________

At this time let us use another tool that can help you along the way. God speaks through nature, and that consist of everything around us.

The symbolism of numbers can be a filter to use. The "science of numbers" is what I like to call it. Remember that everything God made was good.

Science of Numbers

The numbers 1 through 9 have various personality traits which are used by numerologist. The numbers 11 and 22 are very important also, but for the meantime we will keep it simple by keeping our focus on the first set of numbers. To begin this exercise, we must determine your *Life Path* number. A *life path* number shows your talents and abilities that you can use as a guide on your path for this life.

Use the example below to help you determine your life path:

Take a person born on: October 25, 1972
Step one: Add the two digits for month and day individually. Add the four digits for year.
10 /25/1972 = 1+0 / 2+5 /1+9+7+2
Step two: Reduce each to a single digit.
1 / 7 / 19
Continue to combine all numbers for month, day, and year by adding. Continue to reduce until the number is a single digit.
1 / 7 / 1+9=
1 / 7 / 10=

1 / 7 / 1+ 0=

1 + 7 + 1 + 0=

1 + 7 + 1= 9

This person has a life path of a 9.

Now you can look at the characteristics of a 9. The life path number indicates where one may excel or indicate a possible vocation. Look at the list of key words on the pages to follow for each life path number.

Number 1

The person with a life path number of 1 indicates a person who is independent, entrepreneurial, inventive, and strong willed. Challenges often met by people with these characteristics are egotism, conceit, and stubbornness. People with a life path of 1 may become successful as a business owners, public figures, or CEOs due to their leadership qualities and pioneering spirit.

Number 2

A person with life path number of 2 is cooperative, diplomatic, insightful, and sensitive. Challenges often met by people with these characteristics are the tendencies to be overly sensitive. These people fear change and are often hesitant when undergoing new ventures. People with a life path of 2 may be successful as psychologist, counselor, artist, spouse, bookkeeper, and coordinator. They are the peacemakers. They work good in partnerships and also make good friends.

Number 3

People with a life path number of 3 are sociable, creative, imaginative, spontaneous, and fun-loving individuals. They may lack focus and have bouts of laziness. These people leave projects unfinished and often exaggerate on details. People with a life path of 3 may be successful as a writer, musician, or artist because they speak and motivate with ease. They are very encouraging to others.

Number 4

People with life path number of 4 are practical, determined, and reliable individuals. They may be neglectful in other areas of life because work is most important to them. People with a life path of 4 may be close minded, idle and rigid. They need security. These are your planners, lawyers, administrators and accountants. People with this life path excel in these professions because they are traditional and structured in nature.

Number 5

People with a life path number of 5 crave variety and change. These are very unconventional, progressive thinking, sensual, and resourceful individuals. Adversely, people with this life path tend to be overindulgent and restless. They want their freedom but they need stability or they will roam without much direction. People with a life path of 5 may be successful in the entertainment industry. They are the advertisers, salesmen, and designers.

Number 6

People with life path number of 6 are compassionate, giving and nurturing individuals. They are very health-oriented. A few challenges that they will face is often anxiety and the act of giving too much of themselves. This person is all about home and family. As a consequence, these individuals have codependency issues and must often detach themselves emotionally to remedy this habit. People with a life path of 6 are successful as a teachers, counselors, nurses, parents, or health consultants.

Number 7

People with a life path number of 7 are investigative and analytical individuals. They are often very philosophical in thought and spiritual in nature. They are the mystics. People with a life path of 7 tend to be anti-social, egocentric and indecisive. They do best working by themselves. They are distrustful of other people. Interestingly, a people with this life path may be successful as professors, religious leaders, or scientists.

Number 8

People with life path number of 8 are authoritarians and influential. These are people in an executive decision role, the organizer. On the flip side of the coin, people with a life path of 8 can be aggressive, confrontational, and materialistic. They often abuse power. These individuals may be successful as business owners, financial advisors, judges, or contractors. They excel in all business related activity.

Number 9

People with a life path number of 9 are compassionate, romantic, idealistic, and forgiving individuals. These individuals are about all things universal and unifying in cause. They may be successful as an environmentalists, community leaders, and craftsmen. They seek work in any capacity that helps or heals.

The characteristics of these numbers that are align to you can be used during your meditation.

A note on numbers 11 or 22:

These numbers are considered master numbers. Rather than reducing these numbers to a single digit, they remain double digits as they require unique attention.

People with a life path that reduces down fully to an 11 or 22 are said to be endowed with special gifts of high-level inspiration and leadership capabilities, but their lives may also be very paradoxical. The paradox exists due to the fact that people with these life paths aim extremely high for their goals while exerting immeasurable pressure on themselves to succeed. People with this life path lack practicality.

People with a life path number of 11 are highly intuitive. This person is a dreamer and has innate psychic capabilities. With all aspects of persons with a life path of a 2, these individuals are charismatic and diplomatic.

People with a life path number of 22 are called the Master Builder. They have the potential to turn any dream into a reality. Idealistic, self-confident, and ambitious are a few of the characteristics that describe these individuals. The 22 life path is unique because this person has the practicality of a life path 4, but the insight of an 11. Those with a life path of a 22 are meant to be on the world stage. Their potential must not be wasted.

Exercise:

My life path is a _______.

List three things that you will incorporate into your life to live up to your path.

1.
2.
3.

What will you avoid to keep from straying off your path?

"The measure of success is not whether you have a tough problem to deal with, but whether it is the same problem you had last year."
John Foster Dulles

"Trust yourself. Think for yourself. Act for yourself. Speak for yourself. Be yourself. Imitation is suicide."
Marva Collins

"We have all been placed on this earth to discover our own path, and we will never be happy if we live someone else's idea of life."
James Van Praagh

"You make the world a better place by making
yourself a better person."
Scott Sorrell

"We all have dreams. But in order to make dreams
come into reality, it takes an awful lot of determination,
dedication, self-discipline, and effort."
Jesse Owens

Until you commit your goals to paper, you have
intentions that are seeds without soil.
- Author unknown

"Knowing is not enough; we must apply.
Wishing is not enough; we must do."
Johann Wolfgang Von Goethe

QUAD IV

HOW DO I FULFILL MY PURPOSE?

In Quadrant IV, we bring together all the previous areas of focus and begin to execute our mission, our purpose.

> *Habakkuk 2: 1-3*
> *1 I will stand at my watch and station myself on the ramparts; I will look to see what he will say to me, and what answer I am to give to this complaint. 2 Then the Lord replied: "Write down the revelation and make it plain on tablets so that a herald may run with it. 3 For the revelation await an appointed time; it speaks of the end and will not prove false. Though it linger, wait for it; it will certainly come and will not delay.*

The most important thing you can do is to have a plan. In this quadrant we will look at goal setting or establishing your game plan. A goal without a plan is just a wish. The scripture above illustrates the power of putting things in writing; it gives us direction and helps us stay on track. Creating a picture makes it easier for our mind to investigate how to make things happen.

The legendary football coach Lou Holtzs wrote down one hundred nine so called "impossible goals" when he was in his twenties. Some of the goals included having dinner in the White House, meeting the Pope and being awarded "Coach of the Year." Decades later he had accomplished all of these and more. Of his original goals he had achieved 81 of them. It is now time for you to decide what you want which will resonate with who you are.

Let us begin by using the SMART goals technique. This is technique was adapted from Paul J. Meyer's book *Attitude Is Everything* which is highly recommended for the purpose of goal setting. We will utilize the "Creating S.M.A.R.T. Goals" section. S.M.A.R.T. stands for specific, measurable, attainable, realistic, and tangible.

A *specific* goal has a much greater chance of being accomplished than a general goal. To set a specific goal you must answer the six "W" questions*: Who is involved? What do I want to accomplish? Where is it going to happen? When is it going to happen? Upon what requirements and/or constraints will it happen? Why will it happen?*

Who is involved? You must identify who is necessary to make this goal happen. *Is it you? Is it your teammates? Is it your family members?* In order to see the idea to completion you must ask yourself who must be involved. Now that you have assembled the necessary parties, you must establish an objective. *What do you want to accomplish?* Identify a location. Establish a time frame. Identify requirements and constraints. Be specific in the reason, purpose or benefit of accomplishing the goal.

Establish concrete criteria for measuring progress toward the attainment of each goal you set. When you *measure* your progress, it provides you with the ability to stay on track. A measurable goal allows one to reach target dates and deadlines. There is also the sheer exhilaration of achievement that spurs you on and gives you motivation to continue efforts required to reach your overall goal. If your goal is measurable, ask questions such as: *How much? How many? How will I know when it is accomplished?*

You can attain most any goal you set when you plan your steps wisely. Establish a time frame that allows you to carry out those steps towards attainment. Listing goals builds self-image. See yourself as worthy of the goals you list. Develop the traits and characteristics that will allow you to possess the very things you want.

When you identify goals that are most important to you, you begin to figure out ways you can make them come true. You develop the attitudes, abilities, skills, and financial capacity to reach them. You begin seeing previously overlooked opportunities to bring yourself closer to the achievement of your goals. Goals that may have seemed far away and out of reach eventually move closer and become attainable, not because your goals shrink, but because you grow and expand to match them.

To be realistic, a goal must represent an objective toward which you are both willing and able to work. A goal can be both high and realistic; you are the only one who can decide just how high your goal should be. But be sure that every goal represents substantial progress. A high goal is frequently easier to reach than a low one because a low goal exerts low motivational force. Some of the hardest jobs you ever accomplished actually seem easy simply because they were a labor of love.

Your goal is probably realistic if you truly believe that it can be accomplished. Additional ways to know if your goal is realistic is to determine if you have accomplished anything similar in the past or ask yourself what conditions would have to exist to accomplish this goal.

A goal is *tangible* when you can experience it with one of the senses, that is, taste, touch, smell, sight or hearing.

When your goal is tangible, or when you tie a tangible goal to a intangible goal, you have a better chance of making it specific, measurable, and thus attainable.

Intangible goals are your goals for the internal changes required to reach more tangible goals. They are the personality characteristics and the behavior patterns you must develop to pave the way to success in your career or for reaching some other long-term goal. Since intangible goals are vital for improving your effectiveness, give close attention to tangible ways for measuring them.

Exercise:

What is your goal for this month? Next month? In three months?

What is your goal for this year? In five years? In ten years?

Buy a planner. Commit yourself to a schedule Monday through Sunday. Every day include an activity associated with your goals.

Your S.M.A.R.T Goal Exercise:

Specific

Who/what is involved?

Measureable

How much? How many? How will I know when it is accomplished?

Attainable

What is my timeframe?

Relevant

Can I accomplish this in my present position?

Time

What does this goal look like? Taste like? Feel like? Sound like? Smell like?

Sister/Brother, we have come full circle on the wheel of life. It is our hope that you've discovered your true self. You now have a roadmap to keep the design for your life a reflection of your newly defined self.

With this new sense of self, it is also our hope and prayer that, like the birthmark, thumbprint, and snowflake, you relish in your individual contribution to this earth.

Just as your past experience has brought you to this juncture of self awareness, we charge you to plant new seeds of consciousness. Make a conscious effort to meditate and to pause in order to reconnect with our spirit at life's crossroads. We charge you not to turn into a pillar of salt, but into a full blooming rose—whether you are surrounded by blazes of grass or concrete.

We now understand how fear and doubt can paralyze us, so it is our prayer that you act on your lot in life. You now have the tools to not only reflect but to act and execute. You were made with the agreement that you were to use your natural talents and gifts to leave this earth better than you left it. May you walk well on your path and never stray from the commitment you made to this journey and the commitment you made to yourself.

AFFIRMATIONS

"You must try to generate happiness within yourself. If you aren't happy in one place, chances are you won't be happy anyplace."
Ernie Banks

"Attitude is a little thing that makes a big difference."
Winston Churchill

"If you want to feel rich, just count the things you have that money can't buy."
Unknown

"The best way to predict the future is to invent it."
Alan Kay

"The game of life is the game of boomerangs. Our thoughts, deeds and words return to us sooner or later, with astounding accuracy."
Florence Shinn

"Eventually we grow weary of seeking treasures outside ourselves and we begin to look within. There we discover that the gold we sought, we already are."
Alan Cohen

"I think there's a great beauty to having problems. That's one of the ways we learn."
Herbie Hancock

"Do we need more time? Or do we need to be more disciplined with the time we have?"
Kerry Johnson

"Wanting to be someone you're not is a waste of the person you are."
Kurt Cobain

"The kind of beauty I want most is the hard-to-get kind that comes from within - strength, courage, dignity."
Ruby Dee

"Failing doesn't make you a failure. Giving up, accepting your failure, refusing to try again does!"
Richard Exely

"And in the end it's not the years in your life that count. It's the life in your years."
Abraham Lincoln

"It is easy to sit up and take notice, what is difficult is getting up and taking action."
Honore de Balza

"Nothing is too small to know, and nothing is too big to attempt."
William Van Horne

"You are the only person on earth who can use your ability."
Zig Ziglar

"Confidence is contagious. So is lack of confidence."
Michael O'Brien

"It's not where you start - it's where you finish that counts."
Zig Ziglar

"We cannot become what we need to be by remaining what we are."
Max De Pree

"What we see depends mainly on what we look for."
John Lubbock

"If you want to be successful, it's just this simple: Know what you're doing. Love what you're doing. And believe in what you're doing."
Will Rogers

"Mistakes are the portals of discovery."
James Joyce

"Do not wait; the time will never be 'just right.' Start where you stand, and work with whatever tools you may have at your command, and better tools will be found as you go along."
Napleon Hill

"I learned that success and happiness are not values to pursue; they are values to develop."
Jim Rohn

"You were born an original. Don't die a copy."
John Mason

"So many of our dreams at first seem impossible, then they seem improbable, and then, when we summon the will, they soon become inevitable."
Christopher Reeve

"Great things are not done by impulse, but by a series of small things brought together."
Vincent Van Gogh

"What we have to learn to do, we learn by doing."
Aristotle

"Once you replace negative thoughts with positive ones, you'll start having positive results."
Willie Nelson

"Start living now. Stop saving the good china for that special occasion. Stop withholding your love until that special person materializes. Every day you are alive is a special occasion. Every minute, every breath, is a gift from God."
Mary Manin Morrissey

"Our thoughts and imagination are the only real limits to our possibilities."
Orison Swett Marden

"Action is the foundational key to all success."
Pablo Picasso

"I was always looking outside myself for strength and confidence, but it comes from within. It is there all the time."
Anna Freud

"The greatest amount of wasted time is the time not getting started."
Dawson Trotman

"Everything that irritates us about others can lead
us to an understanding of ourselves."
Carl Jung

"There's no secret to getting started. You simply
decide and then take your first step. With each
subsequent step, the nextone becomes easier..."
Tom Venuto

"Success is to be measured not so much by the position that one
has reached in life as by the obstacles which he has overcome."
Booker T. Washington

"Move out of your comfort zone. You can only grow if you are willing
to feel awkward and uncomfortable when you try something new."
Brian Tracy

"Never be bullied into silence. Never allow yourself to be made a
victim. Accept no one's definition of your life; define yourself."
Harvey Fierstein

"Heaven on Earth is a choice you must
make, not a place you must find."
Wayne Dyer

"Be yourself. An original is always worth more than a copy."
Author Unknown

"A goal without a plan is just a wish."
Antoine de Saint-Exupery

"You are today where your thoughts have brought you; you will be tomorrow where your thoughts take you."
James Lane Allen

"I am not a has-been. I am a will be."
Lauren bacall

"One may walk over the highest mountain one step at a time."
John Wanamaker

"Nothing can add more power to your life than concentrating all your energies on a limited set of targets."
Nido Qubein

"If you judge people, you have no time to love them."
Mother Theresa

"You can't base your life on other people's expectations."
Stevie Wonder

One who is in conflict with everyone is the one who is wrong
African Proverb (Wolof people)

"Holding onto anger is like grasping onto a hot coal with the intent of throwing it at someone else. You are the one who gets burned."
Gautama Buddha

Exercise:

Pick one of the affirmations that you want to remember.

Write what this affirmation means to you.

In which areas of your life would you use this affirmation to in order to move closer to your purpose?

Now it's time to create your own affirmations. Use these affirmations to propel you to your destiny. Write it down. Paste it in the bathroom mirror, by the door, or wherever you need it to be placed. This is your wish for yourself.

We will begin with "I AM" statements, then move into a free form.

I AM ____

I AM ____

I AM ____

____

____

www.ingramcontent.com/pod-product-compliance
Ingram Content Group UK Ltd.
Pitfield, Milton Keynes, MK11 3LW, UK
UKHW020233250726
13967UKWH00001B/336

9 781483 406473